For Marion and Alexander
—E.C.

Library of Congress Cataloging-in-Publication Data

Chew, Elizabeth V., 1963–
Thomas Jefferson: A Day at Monticello / by Elizabeth V. Chew.
p. cm.
Includes bibliographical references and index.
ISBN 978-1-4197-0541-0
1.Monticello (Va.)—Juvenile literature. 2.Jefferson, Thomas, 1743–1826—Homes and haunts—Virginia—
Juvenile literature. I. Thomas Jefferson Foundation. II. Title.
E332.74.C55 2013
973.4'6092—dc23
2012010023

Printed and bound in China
10 9 8 7 6 5 4 3 2 1

Abrams Books for Young Readers are available at special discounts when purchased in quantity for premiums and
promotions as well as fundraising or educational use. Special editions can also be created to specification. For
details, contact specialsales@abramsbooks.com or the address below.

MONTICELLO
www.monticello.org

ABRAMS
THE ART OF BOOKS SINCE 1949

115 West 18th Street
New York, NY 10011
www.abramsbooks.com

Contents

Preface . . . iv

A Day with Thomas Jefferson
at Monticello . . . 1

Timeline: Thomas Jefferson
& Monticello . . . 45

Notes . . . 47

Bibliography . . . 48

Acknowledgments . . . 49

Index . . . 49

Portrait of Thomas Jefferson by Thomas Sully (1821).

Preface

THOMAS JEFFERSON (1743–1826) GREW UP IN THE MID-1700S AT SHADWELL, his father's plantation in the hills of central Virginia, one of the British colonies of North America. From his father, Peter Jefferson, he learned about surveying the land, about growing tobacco, and about a society where free white people owned black slaves. Thomas Jefferson was a good student who liked literature, history, math, and science. He was curious about every aspect of the world around him.

When he grew up, Jefferson became a leader in his community. When the American colonies were sending representatives to a Continental Congress in Philadelphia to discuss how the British government was treating them, Jefferson was chosen to go from Virginia. He became part of a team asked to draft a declaration of independence. Because he had a way with words, Jefferson wrote the draft. It said that "all men are created equal" and have "certain unalienable rights," among which are "life, liberty and the pursuit of happiness." Jefferson and his friends created a new nation based on the ideas of equality and self-government. He went on to serve as ambassador to France, secretary of state, vice president, and president of the United States. Although he traveled extensively, met famous people, including royalty, and saw much of Europe when most Americans never strayed far from where they were born, Jefferson often said he would rather be home at Monticello.

As a boy at Shadwell, Jefferson looked across the Rivanna River at a small mountain he called Monticello, an Italian word meaning "little mountain." He dreamed of living on top of that mountain when he grew up, and when he was twenty-five, he started making his dream a reality. He designed and built a house on the mountaintop and lived there with his wife and children. Later, after his wife died, he completely remodeled that first house. It was the center of his large farm—or plantation—and, because of its architecture and gardens, one of the most famous houses in America.

Jefferson's fascination with the world around him continued throughout his life. He was certain that human beings, through reason, could improve their world. He was therefore committed to gathering, recording, and sharing what he called "useful knowledge," information that could make anything in life more efficient, productive, comfortable, or convenient. This book follows Jefferson through one typical day in his life in the spring of 1813.

A DAY WITH THOMAS JEFFERSON AT MONTICELLO

EVERY MORNING, WITH THE FIRST LIGHT OF DAWN, THOMAS JEFFERSON wakes and glances at the clock on the shelf at the bottom of his bed. He rises with the sun and is always curious to know the time and temperature. Mounted on two pieces of wood outside his bedroom window is his thermometer.

It is 46 degrees Fahrenheit—8 degrees warmer than yesterday. Reaching for his pocket notebook, Jefferson spreads the ivory leaves open like a fan and records the temperature on one of the pages. Later in the day he will again record the temperature and the weather conditions.

Once a week, Jefferson transfers these daily notes on the weather into his more official record—the "Weather Memorandum Book." Then he uses a bit of cloth to wipe the ivory book clean for use the next week.

Many years ago, Jefferson devised a system for recording the weather, and now he has accumulated almost forty years' worth of information. He has created a picture of the climate on the mountaintop, from morning to night, day to day, week to week, month to month, and year to year. This is valuable information he hopes to share with a network of other weather watchers throughout the country—fellow scientists

Ivory notebooks.

Recording the Weather

IN THE "WEATHER MEMORANDUM BOOK" EACH page is arranged in a series of columns for recording the day of the month, morning and afternoon temperatures, and weather conditions. Jefferson recorded his observations of weather conditions using the following code: *a* is "after"; *c*, "cloudy"; *f*, "fair"; *h*, "hail"; *r*, "rain"; *s*, "snow." Thus, *c a r h s* means "cloudy after rain, hail, and snow." Precise record keeping was of the utmost importance to Jefferson.

A page from the "Weather Memorandum Book."

eager to develop a theory about the new nation's climate. With this information, people will be better able to plan their lives and work. For instance, farmers will know when to expect the last frost of spring and the first snow of winter; travelers will know when certain trails and roads will be covered in snow and when thaws set in.

Jefferson rings the servants' bell with a lever located next to the fireplace. Burwell Colbert, the enslaved butler at Monticello, is Jefferson's manservant. Jefferson rings every morning when he wakes up. Colbert climbs the steep, narrow stairs up to the bedroom and puts a basin of cold water on the floor near the alcove bed.

"Good morning, sir," says Colbert.

"A fine morning to you, Burwell," replies Jefferson as he sits on the bed to bathe his feet in the ice-cold water. The water basin is always placed on the bedroom side of the bed and in the same place—as a worn mark on the floor reveals. Jefferson believes soaking his feet is good for his health, and it certainly wakes him up. He is in his seventies and has plunged his feet into cold water every morning for as long as he has lived at Monticello.

After the invigorating footbath, Jefferson dresses. At the end of his bed is a special clothes-storage device he designed himself. After visiting Monticello, Augustus John Foster, a British diplomat, wrote, "In a recess at the foot of the bed was a [structure] with forty-eight projecting hands on which hung his coats and waistcoats and which he . . . could turn round with a long stick; a knick-knack that [he] was fond of showing with many other little mechanical inventions."

Jefferson selects stockings, underdrawers (underwear), a shirt, breeches (pants), a waistcoat (vest), and a neck stock (an old-fashioned necktie worn like a band around the neck). He prefers plain, comfortable clothes and does not mind if they are old or out of style. His granddaughter Ellen would later write, "His dress was simple, and adapted to his ideas of neatness and comfort. He paid little attention to fashion, wearing whatever he liked best, and sometimes blending the fashions of several different periods."

Jefferson's alcove bed.

Jefferson's Alcove Bed

THE DESIGN OF THE BED WAS BASED on cozy beds in Europe, like the ones Jefferson saw when he lived in Paris, France, where he served as an American diplomat. He lived there from 1784 to 1789. Some beds in Europe were built into a wall and had only one side open. Jefferson's opened on both sides—one side was his bedroom, and the other was his cabinet, or study.

Jefferson was so interested in measuring and recording information that he even kept records of how warm his layers of covers were in the winter. He used a wolf pelt as one of his winter coverings.

Where Did People Go to the Bathroom?

A privy at Monticello.

IN JEFFERSON'S LIFETIME, PEOPLE DID NOT HAVE RUNNING WATER OR TOILETS THAT flushed. Most people used a chamber pot, a round bowl with a handle, instead of a toilet. In some homes, these were emptied and cleaned by servants or slaves. Indoor places reserved especially for using the chamber pot were rare in the United States, but inside the Monticello house there were three tiny private rooms where the Jefferson family and their visitors could go. Jefferson called them "air-closets." One was located across from the foot of Jefferson's bed and used only by him. The other two were off the south passageway on the first and second floors of the house. There were also two outdoor privies, located at either end of the passageway that ran underneath the house. The outdoor privies held wooden seats over pits that drained into a tunnel in the hillside. Jefferson paid male slaves for completing the unpleasant task of "cleansing sewers," approximately once a month. For example, Edward Gillette, the father of Gill, Israel, Agnes, and Barnaby, was paid to clean the sewers in 1822. (Jefferson kept very accurate records!) A fifth "necessary house" was located on Mulberry Row and was probably for enslaved and hired people who lived and worked there.

After a quick visit to his private privy, or toilet—located in a tiny room just across from the clothes contraption at the end of his bed—Jefferson retreats to his cabinet to write letters until it is time for breakfast.

The cabinet is Jefferson's special office—part of his "sanctum sanctorum," which means his sanctuary or private place. It contains all of his favorite things, and no one may enter without his permission. Jefferson chose the pieces of furniture to create the perfect writing arrangement. Writing letters is very important to him, because letters allow him to stay in contact with his many friends all over the world, as well as his neighbors just a few miles away.

Jefferson puts on his reading spectacles and sits down at his custom-made writing table, complete with a rotating chair, which he can move from side to side as he works. He can

A polygraph machine.

swivel to his right to consult one of the five books on his revolving book stand, or turn to his left to use his microscope.
He can also turn the top of the table around. The chair has
candlesticks on the arms for reading at night. In the center
of Jefferson's desk is one of his favorite machines—a kind
of copier called a polygraph. He thinks the polygraph is
"the finest invention of the present age." When Jefferson
begins to write with one of the pens of the polygraph, the
other pen, connected by wires and wooden levers, makes a
copy of his words.

This is the original letter Jefferson wrote to
granddaughter Cornelia Jefferson Randolph on June
3, 1811. He used his polygraph to make a copy of the
letter and then stored it in his filing press with other
important correspondence.

Dear Sir
Monticello Apr 3.13.
Yours of the 23d Ult. has been duly received . . .

The polygraph copy is identical, though the writing wobbles a bit.

When he is finished, Jefferson folds a letter cover (a piece of paper used like an enve-
lope) around the handwritten letter, seals it by melting some special wax over the opening
and stamping his emblem in it, and sets it aside to mail. Then he carefully takes out the

copy and steps over to a simple wooden cabinet sitting on the floor. He stores all of his letters in these filing cabinets, which he calls filing presses. The filing presses, like the writing table and revolving book stand, were made on the Monticello plantation in the joinery, or woodworking shop. Since Jefferson is an important person and had been the third president of the United States, his letters are often on noteworthy subjects, and he knows people might want to read them in the future. Over the years, his letters have created a record of his life. (Jefferson wrote around 19,000 letters in his entire lifetime and saved copies of nearly all of them!)

Lap desk.

Revolving book stand.

On top of one of the cabinets is a large, flat, rectangular wooden box. When opened, the box becomes a miniature desk itself—one that rests on Jefferson's lap nicely if he is sitting in a chair or in bed. It was on this little desk that Jefferson, when he was thirty-three in 1776, wrote the most famous document in all of American history—the Declaration of Independence.

Jefferson gets settled back at his desk and begins setting up his next project. He puts his "Garden Book" on the revolving book stand, gives it a quarter-turn, and adds *The American Gardener's Calendar* and a dictionary. Jefferson's revolving book stand enables him to keep five books open at once. The stand is handy for a voracious reader like Jefferson. He once told his old friend John Adams that he had a "canine" appetite for reading.

Eek-o, eek-o, eek-o, eek-o, eek-o!

Jefferson leaps up from his chair. In his enthusiasm over his morning work, he has forgotten Dick, his mockingbird, who is eager for some exercise. Dick's cage is in the greenhouse next to the study. As Jefferson opens the glass doors to this space, the southeast piazza, he smells citrus. The greenhouse is a haven for tender plants, those unable to withstand harsh weather, such as acacia, orange, lemon, and lime trees. He walks over to a bamboo cage and unlatches the door. Dick flies out into the greenhouse.

Jefferson's grandchildren love to play with the bird and introduce him to visitors. Dick can even mimic some of Jefferson's favorite tunes. One of them is a Scottish folk song called "Willie Was a Wanton Wag." His friend Alexander Wilson, a famous ornithologist (someone who studies birds), set patriotic words to this tune to make a song called "Jefferson and Liberty."

When author and family friend Margaret Bayard Smith came to stay for a few days, she wrote about the "constant companionship" Dick provided. Whenever Jefferson was alone, she said, "he opened the cage and let the bird follow about the room. After flitting for a while from one object to another, it would alight on his table and regale him with its sweetest notes, or perch on his shoulder and take its food from his lips."

Ding, ding, ding.

Colbert's ringing of the second bell reminds Jefferson that it's time to join the family in the dining room for breakfast. Jefferson opens his bedroom door and strides through the entrance hall to the dining room.

"Good morning, good morning, everyone!" he exclaims, smiling, as he beholds his family and guests sitting at the big oval breakfast table.

At the table are his daughter Martha and her husband, Thomas Randolph, and their children: Jeff (age twenty), Ellen (sixteen), Cornelia (thirteen), Virginia (eleven), Mary (nine), James (seven), Ben (four), and Lewis (three). Also seated are Jefferson's guests, President James Madison and his wife, Dolley. President Madison has taken a holiday away from the capital in Washington, D.C., to stay at his plantation, Montpelier—a distance of about 30 miles from Monticello—and has come to visit. Jefferson and his family often have important and famous visitors. Another visitor is Jefferson's grandson Francis Eppes, age eleven. His mother, Jefferson's daughter Mary Jefferson Eppes, died when Francis was three. He lives with his father and stepmother on his father's plantation in Buckingham

County, about 40 miles away, and often visits his grandpapa, Aunt Martha, Uncle Thomas, and his cousins at Monticello.

Burwell has set out the family's usual morning meal of cold ham and three different kinds of hot bread with butter—wheat and corn breads, plus special Monticello muffins—and coffee for the adults. Monticello muffins are made out of flour, yeast, and water and baked on a griddle over the fire.

"These muffins are a great luxury to me," sighs Jefferson as he sits down. He begins passing around the ham and muffins as Burwell pours the coffee.

Ben Randolph is sitting next to Dolley Madison, a favorite guest of Jefferson's grandchildren. He takes a muffin from the platter and attempts to split it in half. When Mrs. Madison starts to help him cut the muffin with a knife, he puts his hand on hers and exclaims, "No! No! That is not the way!"

"Well, how then, Master Ben?" asks Mrs. Madison.

"Why, you must tear him open and put butter inside and stick holes in his back! And then pat him and squeeze him, and the juice will run out!"

Mrs. Madison fixes herself a muffin as Ben has instructed. "You are right, Ben," she exclaims. "This is the most delicious way to eat a Monticello muffin."

After breakfast the youngest children are tended to by an enslaved woman named Priscilla Hemmings, the wife of John Hemmings, the joiner. The older children do lessons with their mother while Ellen Randolph, who is learning the role of housekeeper, heads downstairs with a large bunch of keys to check on supplies in the storage cellars and talk to the cook, Edith Fossett, about dinner. Jefferson walks President Madison and his wife to the door to say their good-byes, and then the Madisons depart in their carriage for Montpelier.

After finishing more letters and other business at his desk, Jefferson sets out for his daily visits around the plantation. Monticello is not just a house. It is a 5,000-acre working

plantation that consists of four farms—the Monticello home farm, Shadwell, Tufton, and Lego. Slaves work the farms under the supervision of overseers. The slaves and overseers live on the farms where they work. They grow wheat, the main cash crop for Jefferson, and other crops, such as corn, that are used to feed animals.

Jefferson's plow, with its special moldboard.

Jefferson's first stop on his rounds is Mulberry Row, a part of the road that makes a circle around the top of the Monticello mountain. Mulberry Row, the "Main Street" of the plantation, lies just below the south side of the house, near the kitchen, and was named for the mulberry trees planted along it. Some of the slaves who work in the main house live with their families in small log cabins on Mulberry Row. Enslaved artisans also run busy workshops on the row.

"Good day!" he calls to the two enslaved blacksmiths, Joseph Fossett and Moses Hern, as he enters their shop. "How goes the work on my plow?"

The blacksmiths are heating iron over the fire in the forge so they can bend and shape the metal. Jefferson is happy to see that they are attaching a new iron moldboard—the part of the plow that turns over the earth after it is cut—to a wooden plow. The talented blacksmiths have made the special moldboard in their shop. Jefferson designed it—the only thing he ever wholly invented—because he thought that with its curved shape, it would do a better job of turning over the earth than a traditional moldboard. He got the idea when he was traveling in France and saw workers struggling with their plows. He likes seeing his ideas put into practice.

Monticello, showing Mulberry Row, the vegetable garden and orchard, and the fields beyond. Watercolor by Gail McIntosh.

After leaving the blacksmith shop, Jefferson stops in the joinery.

"Good day, Johnny," he exclaims. "What are you making today?"

"The dumbwaiter for your dining room, sir," replies John Hemmings.

"Excellent," says Jefferson. "A dumbwaiter in the dining room holds everything necessary for the progress of the dinner from beginning to end," Jefferson explains, "so we can dine in a comfortable, relaxed style, as the French do."

He touches the rich brown wood from a walnut tree. A hard wood with a beautiful color, walnut is often used for furniture. As Jefferson watches, Hemmings carves a mortise-and-tenon joint to connect one of the horizontal shelf pieces to the vertical leg pieces.

The woodworking and furniture-making shop is called the joinery because the furniture made there is held together mostly with joints rather than nails. The pieces of wood are cut to fit exactly. While Jefferson was remodeling Monticello, Hemmings learned all about building fine houses and making furniture from an Irishman named James Dinsmore, an expert joiner Jefferson hired to supervise his house-remodeling project and run the joinery. Rebuilding Monticello took so long that Dinsmore lived at Monticello for ten and a half years! After Dinsmore left, the skillful Hemmings took over running the joinery and often makes furniture for Jefferson and his family, including filing cabinets, chairs, and tables. The Monticello joinery is an especially well-equipped woodworking shop, containing the largest inventory of tools of any woodshop in Virginia.

Gill Gillette waits outside the joinery with Jefferson's bay horse, Bremo. Gillette is an enslaved groom who cares for Jefferson's horses in the stable at the end of Mulberry Row. He is also a postilion, which means he drives Jefferson's special carriage, called a landau, by riding one of the horses that pulls it. Beside Gillette is Jefferson's grandson Francis, already mounted on a horse named Diomede. Francis is eager to join his grandfather on the plantation rounds today.

Jefferson and Francis ride down Mulberry Row, past the stable, where they join a path leading to the South Spring. On their way down to the overseer's house, they ride past a flock of Barbary broad-tailed sheep grazing under the watchful eye of a young shepherd. Jefferson has experimented with several breeds of sheep, trying to find those with the best meat for eating and the best wool for weaving into cloth.

"Is that a new dog keeping the sheep away from the wheat, Grandpapa?" asks Francis.

"Yes, that is Armandy. The Marquis de Lafayette sent me two of the genuine *chiens de berger*, shepherd's dogs from France. They are the most careful, intelligent dogs in the world—the finest house dogs and farm dogs I know. Would you like a sheepdog puppy? Armandy is having a litter soon."

Francis's eyes grow wide, and a grin spreads across his face. "Thank you, Grandpapa!" he says.

As they ride down the slope of his mountain, Jefferson spots a blue wildflower. He dismounts and kneels to look at the Virginia bluebell, or *Mertensia virginica.* The flower normally blooms around this time, and Jefferson is delighted to see this sign of spring. With his pocket scissors, he clips a bunch of the trumpet-shaped blossoms. He holds them up to show Francis, then reaches into his pocket for his ivory notebook so he can make a notation about their blooming. He has been recording the blooming of spring wildflowers for almost fifty years. He carefully tucks the flowers into a pocket on his saddlebag so he can show the other grandchildren.

About a mile from the mountaintop, Jefferson and Francis arrive at overseer Edmund Bacon's house. Bacon is not a slave. He is a white man who manages the home farm operations and lives in a house on the side of the mountain near the fields where the enslaved workers grow wheat and corn. As Jefferson and Francis ride up, Bacon comes out of the house.

"Good day to you," calls Jefferson. "What news of my wheat crop?"

"The weather has been dry, as you know, sir," says Bacon. "We need a good rain."

Francis listens carefully as the men talk so that he can learn about growing wheat. Someday he may run his grandfather's Poplar Forest plantation, some 90 miles away.

The harvest will begin in a couple of months—toward the end of June. The harvest season is one of the busiest times of the year at Monticello. Jefferson organizes the wheat harvest so that everyone has a particular role. Men, women, and children who do not ordinarily do farmwork join their fellow slaves in the fields, working as mowers, binders, gatherers, stackers, and loaders. Jefferson even assigns enslaved cooks who usually work at the house to prepare meals in the fields.

Francis and his grandfather continue on their rounds, heading toward the river.

Boom! Boom!

"What was that?" Francis exclaims, as he reins in the frightened Diomede.

"The workmen by the river are blasting rock with gunpowder," answers Jefferson.

"Why?" asks the startled Francis.

"To make a canal to bring water to my new mill," replies Jefferson. "They bore holes in the rock and pack in the powder. They then ignite the powder to cause the explosion we just heard. It is important to have superior-quality powder in order to make the work go faster. I ordered some from my friend Mr. Du Pont in Delaware but have not received it. Using the miserable stuff we have here, the workmen have to bore bigger holes, so the work takes longer. We will stop at Milton on the way home to see if the shipment has arrived."

Francis knows that his grandfather prefers things to be done in the quickest and least wasteful way possible.

The road ends at the Rivanna River at the foot of Monticello mountain. The river is the lifeline of the plantation. The wheat crop, ground into flour, goes by boat to markets—such as those in the city of Richmond, Virginia—where it is sold. For this reason the river is very important for Jefferson and other plantation owners. Goods from all around the world arrive by river too. The river port is a little nearby town called Milton. The flowing river also powers Jefferson's mills, which is why the enslaved workers need to blast the rock to make the new canal. Jefferson is very excited to show Francis the progress on his latest mill-construction project. His workmen have almost finished building a mill here in what he calls the River Field.

"This is not an ordinary mill," explains Jefferson.

"What will it be able to do?" asks Francis.

"It will saw logs into boards for building, thresh wheat by separating the wheat kernels from their chaff, remove the corn kernels from corncobs, and grind the wheat and corn kernels into flour and cornmeal. We will use some of the flour at Monticello and send the rest to market. The mill can also separate the hemp plant into fibers for making rope

The Rivanna River allowed travel by flatboat to carry goods to town.

or clothing for the slave children," replies his grandpapa with pride. "And all this may be done using just one waterwheel to provide the power!"

"That is amazing!" declares Francis. "I can't believe that one machine can do so many different jobs."

"And the new canal will redirect water from the river to turn the waterwheel. But it has been a problem getting enough water to turn the wheel. The weather has been very dry, making the river low. So far, the only part of the mill that works is the sawmill for cutting logs into boards for building. This, however, is better than before, when logs were sawed by hand at the end of Mulberry Row near the joinery."

"Good day, sir!" calls John Brown, walking up from the mill. He is the millwright in charge of building the mill. "I had hoped you were men from Milton with the gunpowder. Without it we will not get the mill running anytime soon."

"My friend Du Pont says he dispatched it," Jefferson replies. "Francis and I will stop at Milton again today to inquire about the shipments."

Bremo and Diomede carry Jefferson and Francis across the Rivanna to Shadwell Farm on the other side. They turn left to go upstream and westward along the river toward Lego Farm. Lego is currently the site of Monticello's spinning and weaving operations.

As they approach the textile factory, a man steps outside to greet them.

"Here is William Maclure, whom I have hired to organize the factory and teach the slaves to use the machinery," Jefferson tells Francis.

Maclure ushers the guests into the textile workshop. Francis is impressed with the busy shop and the whirring and thumping machines that the enslaved women and children are running. They make cloth from the wool, flax, and hemp produced on the plantation and from the cotton purchased by Jefferson. Jefferson distributes cloth or clothing to all the slaves twice a year.

"What are all the different machines used for?" Francis asks Maclure.

"Ah, I see you have the curiosity of your grandfather. Come look," says Maclure, leading them around the shop. "Israel here is feeding in the wool and turning the handle of the drum carding machine. It untangles and straightens the clumps of wool sheared off the sheep, so the spinners can use it." Francis recognizes Israel Gillette, who is almost exactly his age. Israel is the younger brother of Gill, the stable groom. Francis and Israel went on a bird-hunting trip together during Francis's Christmastime visit.

"How long will you work today, Israel?" asks Francis. "Perhaps we may hunt again."

Israel hesitates and looks down. "Until sundown," he says softly.

Slavery

JEFFERSON'S WORDS ABOUT SLAVERY did not match his actions on his Monticello plantation. Though he wrote in the Declaration of Independence that "all men are created equal" and said that slavery was an "abominable crime," his livelihood depended on the labor of people he held in slavery. At any one time, there were as many as 130 men, women, and children living and working in slavery at Monticello, running the house, the four farms, gardens, and workshops for the Jefferson family. Jefferson freed only nine slaves during his lifetime or in his will. By the end of his life he came to believe that abolishing slavery was the work of a future generation. His grandson Francis Eppes inherited property, including slaves, from his grandfather. Although he did free at least one person, Eppes did not free all his slaves. Slavery did not end in the United States until the Thirteenth Amendment to the Constitution abolished it at the end of the Civil War in 1865, thirty-nine years after Jefferson's death.

"But that's twelve hours!" exclaims Francis.

Maclure moves on. Harriet Hemings and Agnes Gillette, Gill and Israel's sister, are spinning cotton on the spinning jennies. These machines use multiple spindles for spinning.

"How much yarn can the spinning jennies make?" asks Francis.

"With our twenty-four-spindle jenny, Harriet can spin two pounds of cotton yarn a day. That's four times as much as she could do on the old spinning wheel," replies Maclure. "And as the final step in the textile-making process, Mary Hern and Dolly weave the yarn into cloth on these looms with flying shuttles."

"Do the shuttles really fly?" asks Francis.

"No, but they make the work go much faster," says Maclure, laughing.

"Farewell and thank you," says Francis.

As he and his grandpapa ride downstream along the river, Francis asks, "Why is it that I have the time to study and to play with my cousins and to ride with you, sir, while Israel must run the drum carding machine from sunrise to sunset?"

Jefferson sighs, looks at his grandson, and says, "There is nothing I would not give for a workable plan for ending slavery. I believe it is evil and threatens the future of our country."

"Then why do we still have slaves?"

"Here in the southern states," his grandfather begins, "slavery is part of the whole system of life. Ending it will require time, patience, and dedication. I am an old man. I have lived longer than most of my friends with whom I founded our country. The work of ending slavery is for the young—for those who can follow it up and see it through. I hope that you, Francis, and your generation will accomplish this most important work."

They leave Lego Farm and head to Shadwell. Francis has heard many times that Shadwell was the center of his great-grandfather Peter Jefferson's plantation and his grandfather's boyhood home. The house where Thomas Jefferson grew up burned down many years ago, but slaves still farm the fields. The complex includes nine buildings: two mills, two houses for millers, two granaries for storing grain, two coopers' shops (a cooper makes or repairs wooden casks or tubs), and a stable. One of the mills grinds wheat and corn into flour and cornmeal for use at Monticello. The larger mill is rented to millers who grind wheat into flour for Jefferson and other farmers in the area to sell. The flour is packed in wooden barrels and sent down the river in boats to be sold at market in Richmond.

They soon arrive at the Shadwell mill site and stop first at the cooper's shop. One cooper is enslaved Barnaby Gillette,

How Do We Know the Names of Enslaved Workers at Monticello?

THE NAMES OF MANY PEOPLE WHO lived in slavery in the United States have not survived. The names and life stories of slaves at Monticello are known from several different sources, however. Jefferson and his family members referred to enslaved individuals in letters. In his "Farm Book," Jefferson regularly made lists of the slaves working on his four farms, recording only their first names and years of birth and death. He also kept lists of when cloth (for making clothes) and other provisions were distributed to slaves, again listing them by just their first names. Referring to slaves by only their first names was common and helped to reinforce the fact that they were considered property, not individuals. (A slave would never call a white person by his or her first name.) Historians at Monticello have located and interviewed many descendants of people who lived in slavery at Monticello to learn about their family histories, including the last names of many families.

Broken cutlery and dinnerware found where the slave quarters had been located.

Slaves as Consumers

MANY SLAVES ON JEFFERSON'S plantations and farms earned money. Some received tips from visitors. Others got work incentives from Jefferson, like the one he offered to Barnaby Gillette. Jefferson paid others for doing particularly dirty jobs like cleaning out the privies. Many slaves kept their own gardens and chickens and sold vegetables and eggs to the Jefferson family. Slaves spent the money they earned in shops in the nearby town of Charlottesville, where they could walk on Sundays. They bought dishes, teacups, glasses, metal buttons, needles, pins, and scissors. Archaeologists have found the remains of these items around the houses where slaves lived. The record books of some shopkeepers also tell that slaves came into their shops to make purchases. By earning enough money to become consumers, slaves were able to improve their lives.

an older brother of Gill, Israel, and Agnes. He constructs barrels out of wood with metal hoops, and Jefferson sells them to the millers.

"I promise to give you one barrel for every thirty-one you send to the mill," Jefferson tells Gillette. He hopes this plan will encourage Gillette to work even harder and make even more barrels. Though a slave, he can sell the barrels he "earns" and pocket the profit.

"Thank you, sir," says Barnaby. "I will not disappoint you."

"Good afternoon!" Jefferson and Francis call to the miller as they arrive at the mill, next in line in their visits.

When the mill was built, Jefferson had the millwright install the latest machinery so that the milling process would be automated, like a factory. This meant that fewer workers were needed to grind Jefferson's and his neighbors' wheat faster and produce cleaner, better flour. Flour is very important, since it is the main ingredient in bread and other basic foods. The river water turns the waterwheels, and this provides the power that turns gears in the mill's basement. The gears rotate the millstones and turn a main shaft that powers the rest of the machinery in the mill.

"How did you know about this amazing mill machinery?" asks Francis, impressed that the whole mill can be run by only two men.

"I read about it in Oliver Evans's book on his inventions,"

explains Jefferson. "And I paid Mr. Evans patent fees for the right to use his conveyors, elevators, and the rest. I supervised the U.S. Patent Office when I was secretary of state, but I do not approve of patents. I believe in the free sharing of new ideas. I believe that he who receives an idea from me receives instruction himself, without lessening mine; as he who lights his candle at mine receives light without darkening me."

Francis thinks his grandfather is very wise.

Looking across the river to his Tufton Farm on the other side, Jefferson and Francis can see Davy Hern, making charcoal. Blacksmiths at Monticello use charcoal to heat iron in their shop. Cooks Edith Fossett and Frances Hern, Davy's wife, use charcoal for cooking on the stew stoves in the Monticello kitchen. Like many things

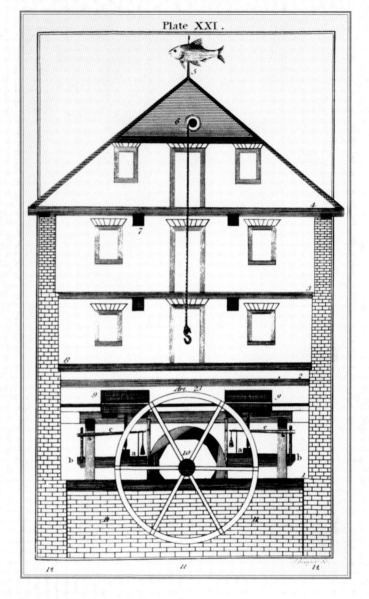

Oliver Evans's design for a flour mill.

on the plantation, charcoal is not available in stores. To make—or "burn"—the charcoal, Davy Hern stacks many wooden sticks into the shape of a dome, leaving an opening in the top. He then covers the sticks with turf—slabs of dirt cut from the ground with the grass still growing on them—and sets the dome on fire from the bottom. Hern must watch this fire carefully day and night so that it burns very slowly and does not spread. After the turf and wood burn, what remains is charcoal, the dark, dry, crumbly leftovers of the sticks.

After leaving the mill site, Jefferson and Francis ride farther downstream before crossing the river again at the little town of Milton. They tie up their horses at David Higginbotham's store to ask about the keg of gunpowder and other things Jefferson is expecting. He often arranges for his shipments that arrive by boat to be delivered to Higginbotham's store, since his house is so far from the river. Jefferson has been waiting more than three months for the shipment from Mr. Du Pont.

"Greetings to you, my friend," says Jefferson as he and Francis enter the store. "My grandson Francis Eppes accompanies me today."

"Good day, gentlemen," says Higginbotham.

"Has my shipment of gunpowder from Mr. Du Pont arrived yet?" asks Jefferson.

"No gunpowder, to my knowledge," says Mr. Higginbotham, "but you did receive a crate yesterday." He leads them into his storeroom at the back of the shop.

"Aha!" exclaims Jefferson, delighted to see that the crate contains two of his favorite things: olive oil and macaroni, which have come all the way from France. "We were out of salad oil, and it is a necessity of life for me. And we will have macaroni with cheese sauce for dinner!"

"There is also this small parcel," says Higginbotham.

Jefferson opens the parcel to discover a book. Looking around the room, he spies some shipping containers partially covered by a canvas cloth in a corner. Pulling back the canvas, Jefferson sees his friend's name on one of the containers. He exclaims, "Here is the gunpowder shipped to me by Mr. Du Pont!"

"I do beg your pardon, Mr. Jefferson. Those containers were left by a waterman nearly three months ago," says Higginbotham. "He provided no instruction, so I did not know where to send them."

"And I have awaited the shipment all this time," laments Jefferson. "I will send someone to retrieve the powder and crate," he tells Higginbotham as he and Francis leave the store. He tucks the book, the macaroni, and the bottle of olive oil into his saddlebag.

Jefferson and Francis set off on the familiar three-mile ride from Milton back to the base of Monticello mountain. Partway there, Jefferson stops and pulls out his pocket sextant.

"You must work hard at your mathematics," he tells his grandson. "It is exciting to use mathematics to measure and learn about our Virginia landscape." Jefferson demonstrates to Francis how to measure the meridian altitude of the sun. Later, in his study, he will continue the instruction, showing Francis how to use the measurements to calculate the latitude of Monticello.

They again ride their horses up the East Road, through open fields, to the Mulberry

Row stable. There Gill Gillette unsaddles Bremo and Diomede and gives them a rubdown.

"You were a good observer and a careful student on our ride today," Jefferson tells Francis, who beams at the praise. "I will see you at dinner."

Jefferson ends his plantation rounds by strolling through his vegetable garden to check on its progress. He stops to admire a small, shiny green bush covered with tiny red peppers. These bird peppers are flourishing at Monticello. He received the hot-pepper seeds from Dr. Samuel Brown, an old friend living in Mississippi. Jefferson keeps up with the world of plants by exchanging information with his network of pen pals, both in the United States and across the Atlantic Ocean. Fellow gardeners regularly send him seeds or plant cuttings, which he experiments with at Monticello. If something does not grow, he records the information and moves on to another experiment. As he says, "The failure of one thing is repaired by the success of another." He keeps careful records—and has since he was a young man—of what he plants, when and where he plants it, how it grows, and his favorite detail: when it is ready to come "to table" so that he and his family and guests can eat it. This experimental method has helped Jefferson grow one of the most diverse gardens ever known in North America.

Peas are always the first vegetable he sows each year. He loves fresh spring peas and competes with his friends to see who can be the first to bring peas to table. And today what does he see? Peas! Not a full crop, but enough for a first harvest. He will serve these first peas to his friend and gardening rival George Divers, who is coming with his wife to dine today. Won't he be surprised!

Next Jefferson inspects his sea kale, a very unusual plant. Sea kale originally came from the seacoasts of Great Britain. Nearby, Jefferson spots the enslaved gardener Wormley Hughes, Burwell Colbert's brother, weeding around some spinach that looks ready for today's dinner table. Jefferson can hardly wait! "Please pick some spinach for dinner to go

with the peas," he says to Hughes. "I am delighted to see it. As you know, vegetables constitute my principal diet." Some vegetables that he plants year after year include peas, sea kale, lettuce and other salad greens, tomatoes, beans, cabbage, asparagus, artichokes, and cucumbers. Jefferson likes salad dressing made from olive oil or sesame oil. Just yesterday, Hughes planted some benne, or sesame, plants. Jefferson hopes to make sesame oil at Monticello so that he no longer has to wait for the shipments to arrive at Milton. "Wormley, please sow some nasturtium seeds as well," he instructs the gardener. Nasturtium leaves add a peppery flavor to salads.

After walking up the path that connects the garden to the main house, Jefferson stops in the kitchen to deliver the macaroni and olive oil. He hands them to the enslaved head cook, Edith Fossett.

"The macaroni and oil were at Milton," he says, "and Wormley is bringing some spinach and peas."

"We'll make macaroni with cheese sauce, sir," says Fossett, "and fresh spinach with the peas and salad dressed with olive oil."

"Delicious," says Jefferson.

Edith Fossett, Frances Hern, and their assistants work busily, preparing the main late-afternoon meal for Jefferson and his family. They cook in one of the more modern kitchens in Virginia. They have a collection of French copper pots and pans as well as a stew stove. In the stew stove burners they use charcoal, so that they can control the amount

Food from Across the Ocean

ALTHOUGH MOST PEOPLE IN THE early United States ate only things that grew or were made close to where they lived, Jefferson learned to enjoy many foods from Europe while he was living there. After he returned home from Paris, France, in 1789, Jefferson regularly placed orders for things that were not produced in America at that time. These included olive oil, wine, raisins, Parmesan cheese, almonds, and "macaroni," the word he used to refer to all kinds of pasta.

of heat. Most cooks at this time use an open fireplace, and the flames are more difficult to control. However, Fossett and Hern prepare the food in what is known as "the French style," and this requires that they braise, or cook, meats slowly over low heat and create delicate, delicious sauces. The two cooks studied with a French chef in Washington while Jefferson was president.

At midafternoon Jefferson is expecting a visit from his friends George and Martha Divers. They live at a nearby plantation called Farmington; Jefferson helped them design an addition to their house a few years ago. Jefferson hurries up to the south terrace and enters his rooms through the open door of the greenhouse, greeting his bird Dick with a cheerful whistle. Pouring water from a pitcher into a basin on his marble-top commode, or cabinet, he washes his hands and face after the long ride. He changes into a clean shirt and

hastens out into the entrance hall. Colbert has greeted and welcomed the Diverses, and now Jeff Randolph and Francis are showing them their grandfather's collections displayed in the tall, two-story room.

George Divers is an eager gardener, like Jefferson, and they often trade seeds, plants, and stories.

"Good afternoon, my friends," says Jefferson, as he enters the hall. "I see that my grandsons are excellent hosts. I believe you have seen the articles in my Indian Hall, the tokens of friendship that Captains Lewis and Clark received from the western tribes."

Jefferson loves showing his collections to visitors. Even those who have visited before can discover something new to see, or hear Jefferson tell a different story about its source or how it came to him. "This buffalo robe, painted by a member of the Mandan tribe, depicts a battle between the Mandan and the Arikara. Our explorers received it as a gift from the hospitable Mandan, who helped them over their difficult first winter." He points out a set of enormous elk

The Lewis and Clark Expedition

LONG BEFORE HE BECAME PRESIDENT, JEFFERSON HAD dreamed of sending explorers across North America. When he took office, he decided to make his dream a reality. On January 18, 1803, President Jefferson sent a confidential letter to Congress asking for $2,500 to fund an expedition to the Pacific Ocean. He hoped to establish trade with the Native American people of the West and find a water route to the Pacific. He sent his personal secretary, Meriwether Lewis, Lewis's friend William Clark, and a group of explorers across the continent. He wrote careful instructions for Lewis:

The object of your mission is to explore the Missouri river, & such principal stream of it, as, by its course & communication with the waters of the Pacific ocean, may offer the most direct & practicable water communication across this continent, for the purposes of commerce.

From the beginning, the encounters between the expedition party and the indigenous (native) people they met were the most significant aspects of the mission. These were the political, diplomatic, and social interactions through which Jefferson's goals of expanding trade and coming to know and understand the inhabitants of the continent were to be forged. Jefferson was also fascinated by the prospect of what could be learned about the geography of the West, the lives and languages of the Native Americans, and how the plants and animals, soil, rocks, and weather differed from those in the East.

antlers on the wall, also from that expedition. Francis loves to imagine the gigantic elk that grew those antlers, as well as the huge moose whose antlers hang nearby.

While he was president, Jefferson had asked Meriwether Lewis and William Clark to explore the American West. He made sure the explorers were trained to record geography, the lives and cultures of native people, and details of soil, plants, animals, minerals, fossils, and climate. The information the explorers recorded in their journals helped people understand more about the American continent. Jefferson is happy that their journals will soon be published as a book.

The Diverses comment on the framed picture hanging over the fireplace. It shows artist John Trumbull's depiction of July 4, 1776.

"Please tell us again about the first Fourth of July," urges Francis, who never gets tired of the story.

"It was a momentous day," Jefferson recalls. "On the fourth, we adopted the Declaration of Independence. I had written the draft during the final two weeks of June. John Dunlap printed the document to distribute to the various states that same day. We had high hopes for the union we were creating, and it brings me great happiness to know that it endures."

Jefferson then escorts them into his Book Room, or library. "I cannot live without books," he says. Jefferson is interested in every subject under the sun—from architecture to zoology—and he has the books to prove it. In fact, he owns about 7,000 volumes in total! His library is one of the most extensive in America. He believes that through learning and gaining knowledge, people can govern themselves, solve all kinds of problems, and improve the world around them.

"Burwell, please call Virginia, Mary, and James into the library," says Jefferson. "I have a special surprise for them." He holds the book he has brought from Milton, a collection of children's stories called *The Parent's Assistant.*

Jefferson's Book Room at Monticello.

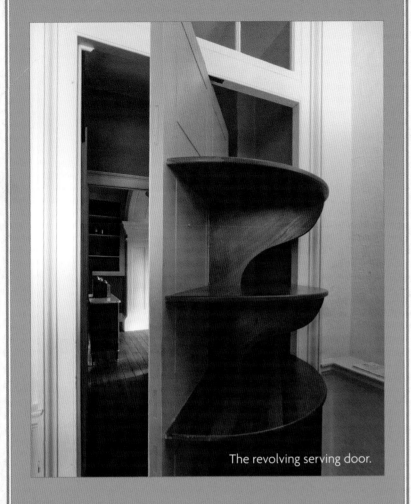
The revolving serving door.

Service

BURWELL COLBERT AND HIS HELPERS ARRANGED THE serving dishes of food on the big dining table in an attractive, symmetrical pattern, but they did not have to carry them all the way up from the kitchen downstairs. The cooks and their assistants brought the dishes of food up from the warming kitchen below and placed them on the shelves of a rotating serving door located in an alcove in a corner of the dining room. Colbert turned the door around, and the dishes of food arrived without interruptions from servers going in and out of the room. He and the waiters could set up the first course and bring in the later courses without a lot of commotion.

When they gather, Virginia excitedly reminds Francis about their tradition: "We draw lots, and whoever draws the longest straw has the first reading of the book; the next longest straw entitles the drawer to the second reading; the shortest, to the last reading *and* ownership of the book." Like their grandfather, the children love to read.

Just before dinner, Jefferson slips into his bedroom to record the temperature again. It is 59 degrees—exactly the same as yesterday at this time and 14 degrees cooler than it was three days ago! Spring is getting off to a slow start.

It is now four in the afternoon. Colbert rings the bell to announce that dinner is served. Hearing the summons, Jefferson returns to the library. He and his grandchildren escort his guests into the dining room, where they are joined by the rest of the large family.

Once seated, they savor the French cuisine. Edith Fossett and Frances Hern have cooked two types of meat—beef and mutton—as well as some fish caught in the Rivanna River and the macaroni with cheese sauce. It is typical to have more than one main dish for dinner.

The cooks have also prepared a variety of garden vegetables, including the spinach, as well as a green salad dressed in olive oil—and, of course, the peas.

"My friend, I salute you and your delicious peas," says George Divers enthusiastically. "You have won! May the competition continue for many years!"

There are not very many peas, barely more than a spoonful for each person, but Jefferson is proud to have brought them to table so early in the spring.

While they eat, Jefferson engages everyone in lively conversation. Gesturing toward the tall window overlooking the lawn and flower garden, he quizzes his younger grandchildren about the paintings and prints hanging beside it. The works of art show some of the impressive natural features of North America. "What do we have in Virginia to rival the falls of Niagara?" he asks.

"The Natural Bridge and the passage of the Potomac through the Blue Ridge," blurts James Randolph before his sisters or brothers can answer, pointing at two prints of the naturally occurring landscapes hanging there.

"Indeed," says Jefferson, "Natural Bridge is one of the most sublime of nature's works, and the joining of the Potomac and Shenandoah Rivers at Harpers Ferry is also one of the most stupendous scenes in nature." Jefferson is always eager to celebrate the United States and American people, animals, and natural beauty.

For dessert the group enjoys different flavors of custards, or puddings, including chocolate and lemon. Afterward, Colbert clears the table, removes the tablecloth, and serves wine to the adults. The group then retires to the parlor.

At seven thirty, Priscilla Hemmings comes to collect the youngest children. She enters from the entrance hall through double glass doors. When she opens one side of the door, the other side opens automatically. This makes it easier to open the door if she is carrying three-year-old Lewis. The doors work via a mechanism similar to a bicycle chain under the threshold. Lewis, Ben, and James, protesting that they are not sleepy, say good night to the family and head upstairs. After bidding their children good night, Martha and Thomas Randolph converse with the Diverses. The guests will spend the night, since travel after dark is difficult.

Ellen, Cornelia, Virginia, and Mary gather their chairs around the fireplace on this cool evening and reach for their books, while Francis and Jeff take up a game of chess. Jefferson relaxes in his favorite chair—the Campeachy—and admires what he calls his circle of readers. The Campeachy is sometimes known as a siesta chair ("siesta" means "nap" in Spanish). Jefferson finds the low chair very comfortable because he can lean back and stretch out his legs. The name Campeachy comes from the port city of Campeche, Mexico, where the chairs were originally made.

At nine o'clock, Jefferson rises and bids good night to his guests. Although he cherishes the evening hours spent with his family and friends, he always looks forward to retiring to his private rooms at the day's end.

Jefferson's Campeachy chair.

This evening he goes to the library to browse through a volume of Latin poetry. With the lines still in his mind, he wanders into the greenhouse and peers at the moon. Dick is asleep in his cage. Jefferson quietly closes the double doors of the greenhouse for the night and continues on to his cabinet. The "Memorandum Book" on his desk reminds him of some unfinished business. He moves an oil lamp onto the desk and lights it. Then he takes the ivory notebook from his pocket and spreads out its leaves. Accounting notes from the past few days have begun to accumulate.

He carefully records his notes in the "Memorandum Book." Then he cleans the ivory leaves with a bit of cloth until they are white again.

This duty completed, Jefferson yawns and extinguishes the flame of his oil lamp. He carries a single candle to his bedroom. By this feeble light, he puts on his nightshirt and nightcap and climbs into the alcove bed. It's ten o'clock now. For the next half hour or more, Jefferson reads from a favorite book by candlelight. This is a time he likes to spend with his own thoughts. He needs something "whereon to ruminate in the intervals of sleep." Even in his dreams, Jefferson imagines himself thinking! He blows out the candle and drifts off to sleep, wondering what the next day will bring.

Aerial view of the west side of Monticello, showing the house, Mulberry Row, the vegetable garden, and orchards.

Timeline: Thomas Jefferson & Monticello

1735: Peter Jefferson, a tobacco planter and a surveyor, acquires 1,000 acres along the Rivanna River in the central part of the Virginia Colony, including the future site of Monticello. He is one of the first settlers in this region. He names his plantation Shadwell after the London parish where his wife, Jane Randolph Jefferson, was born.

1743: Thomas Jefferson is born at Shadwell. He is the third child and first son of eight children.

1748–52: Between the ages of five and nine, Thomas Jefferson lives at Tuckahoe, a plantation about 50 miles from Shadwell, where Peter Jefferson serves as guardian to the children of William Randolph, his friend and his wife's cousin.

1750–60: Jefferson studies with local teachers, learning to read Latin and Greek, essential for a well-educated person of the time.

1757: Peter Jefferson dies.

1760–62: Thomas Jefferson attends the College of William & Mary in Williamsburg. He studies mathematics and natural philosophy (science) with Scottish scholar William Small, who teaches him about the values of the Enlightenment—that the human condition can be improved by reason and knowledge.

1762: Jefferson studies law in Williamsburg with George Wythe.

1764: Jefferson comes into his inheritance from his father at age twenty-one, acquiring about 3,000 acres of land and fifty slaves.

1767–68: Jefferson practices law. He is admitted before the General Court in Williamsburg and elected to the House of Burgesses, the colonial legislature.

1769–70: Jefferson begins leveling Monticello mountain with hired slave labor and constructs a two-room brick building, later remodeled and called the South Pavilion. The house at Shadwell, still home to Jefferson's mother, burns to the ground.

1770: Jefferson moves to the South Pavilion, then the only structure on Monticello mountain, while free and enslaved workers build the main house.

1772: Jefferson marries Martha Wayles Skelton on January 1. Their daughter Martha is born in September.

1773: Martha Jefferson's father, John Wayles, dies. The Jeffersons inherit 11,000 acres and 135 slaves, including Elizabeth (Betty) Hemings and her children.

1774: Jefferson writes *A Summary View of the Rights of British America*, arguing that British colonists in America have the same rights, including representation, as all British citizens. Daughter Jane born.

1775: Jefferson is elected to the Second Continental Congress. Daughter Jane dies.

1776: The Second Continental Congress in Philadelphia names a committee of five—Jefferson, Benjamin Franklin, John Adams, Robert Livingston, and Roger Sherman—to draft a declaration of independence. Jefferson is the primary author. He is elected to the Virginia House of Delegates and appointed to revise Virginia laws. Jefferson's mother, Jane Randolph Jefferson, dies.

1777: As a member of the Virginia House of Delegates, Jefferson drafts *An Act for Establishing Religious Freedom*, setting forth the importance of the separation of church and state. An unnamed son is born and dies.

1778: Jefferson writes *A Bill for the More General Diffusion of Knowledge*, a plan for public education in Virginia. Brickwork for the first Monticello completed. Daughter Mary born.

1779–81: Jefferson serves as governor of Virginia.

1780: Jefferson begins work on what becomes his only book, *Notes on the State of Virginia*. Daughter Lucy Elizabeth born.

1781: During the American Revolution, British troops arrive at Monticello, but Jefferson and his family, warned by a young man named Jack Jouett, have left. Daughter Lucy Elizabeth dies.

1782: Second daughter named Lucy Elizabeth born. Martha Jefferson dies.

1783: The first Monticello house is mostly completed. British General Cornwallis surrenders at Yorktown; the American Revolution ends. Jefferson is elected to the U.S. Congress.

1784: Daughter Lucy Elizabeth dies.

1784–89: Jefferson lives in Paris, first as a commissioner to negotiate trade treaties, then as minister to the court of Louis XVI at Versailles. Daughters Martha and Mary and slaves James and Sally Hemings join him in France. Jefferson visits other regions of France as well as England, Italy, Germany, and the Netherlands. He sees Roman ruins in southern France, English gardens, and art collections, and he investigates details of agriculture and transportation.

1787: Jefferson publishes *Notes on the State of Virginia*.

1790: Upon her return from France, daughter Martha Jefferson marries Thomas Mann Randolph Jr.

1790–93: Jefferson serves as first U.S. secretary of state.

1793–96: Jefferson retires to Monticello and spends three years focused on his farms. He and other planters switch from tobacco to wheat, which requires plowing. Jefferson designs a more efficient plow moldboard. Establishes the nailery on Mulberry Row, run by enslaved boys. Frees manservant Robert Hemings.

1796: Work begins on remodeling and enlarging of Monticello, based on ideas Jefferson brought from France. Jefferson frees chef James Hemings.

1797: Mary Jefferson marries John Wayles Eppes.

1797–1801: Jefferson returns to public life to serve as John Adams's vice president.

1801–9: Jefferson serves as third president of the United States. Returns to Monticello for visits in the spring and summer.

1803: Lewis and Clark Expedition launched. Louisiana Purchase concluded.

1804: Mary Jefferson Eppes dies.

1806: Lewis and Clark Expedition concludes. Work begins on Jefferson's house at Poplar Forest.

1807: Shadwell merchant mill completed.

1809: Jefferson retires from the presidency after two terms and returns to Monticello to live. Remodeling of Monticello and construction of dependencies largely completed. Vegetable-garden terrace completed. Daughter Martha Jefferson Randolph and her large family move to Monticello from their neighboring plantation, Edgehill.

1815: Jefferson sells his library to Congress.

1817: Jefferson begins to realize his plans for a state university dedicated to the "illimitable freedom of the human mind." He designs its neoclassical buildings, hires its professors, and chooses books for its library. Central College (now the University of Virginia) opens for classes in 1825.

1826: Jefferson dies at Monticello on July 4, fifty years to the day after the adoption of the Declaration of Independence.

Notes

For the sake of the reader, dialogue has been created for ease of understanding. Actual quotations and excerpts are noted here.

Page 3 "In a recess at the foot . . ." Augustus John Foster, *Jeffersonian America: Notes on the United States of America, Collected in the Years 1805–6–7 and 11–12.* (San Marino, CA: Huntington Library, 1954), 144.

Page 3 "His dress was simple . . ." Ellen Randolph Coolidge to Henry S. Randall, 1857, in Henry S. Randall, *The Life of Thomas Jefferson* (New York: Derby & Jackson, 1858), 391–92.

Page 5 "the finest invention . . ." Jefferson to James Bowdoin, July 10, 1806, Thomas Jefferson Papers, Library of Congress.

Page 7 "canine" appetite for reading. Jefferson to John Adams, May 17, 1818, in Lester J. Cappon, ed., *The Adams–Jefferson Letters* (Chapel Hill: University of North Carolina Press, 1959), 2:524.

Page 8 "constant companionship." Gaillard S. Hunt, ed., *The First Forty Years of Washington Society: Portrayed by the Family Letters of Mrs. Samuel Harrison Smith (Margaret Bayard)*

from the Collection of Her Grandson, J. Henley Smith (New York: Scribner, 1906), 385.

Page 10 "These muffins are . . ." Thomas Jefferson to Martha Jefferson Randolph, Nov. 2, 1802, in Edwin Morris Betts and James Adam Bear Jr., eds., *The Family Letters of Thomas Jefferson* (University of Virginia Press, 1986), 239.

Page 10 "You are right, Ben . . ." Family story recorded in the memoirs of Jefferson's great-granddaughters, Ellen Wayles Randolph Harrison and Martha Jefferson Trist Burke, *Monticello "Child Life"—Memories of What We Heard from Our Parents*, manuscript, Jefferson Library, Thomas Jefferson Foundation.

Page 10 On the spelling of *Hemings* and *Hemmings*. In spelling his name, John Hemmings, along with his wife, Priscilla, often used a double *m*, while most family members used a single *m*.

Page 27 "I believe that he who receives an idea . . ." Jefferson to Isaac McPherson, Monticello, August 13, 1813, *The Papers of Thomas Jefferson, Retirement Series*, 6:379.

Page 30 "The failure of one thing . . ." Jefferson to Charles Willson Peale, Aug. 20, 1811, *The Papers of Thomas Jefferson: Retirement Series*, 4:93.

Page 33 "As you know, vegetables constitute . . ." Jefferson to Dr. Vine Utley, March 21, 1819, Thomas Jefferson Papers, Library of Congress.

Page 35 "The object of your mission is to explore . . ." Jackson, Donald Dean, ed. "Jefferson's Instructions to Lewis 20 June 1803." *Letters of the Lewis and Clark Expedition with Related Documents, 1753–1854.* (Urbana: University of Illinois Press, 1978), 61–66. (Originally from the Jefferson Papers held by the Library of Congress.)

Page 36 "I cannot live without books." Jefferson to John Adams, June 10, 1815, in *The Adams–Jefferson Letters*, 2:443.

Page 38 "We draw lots, and whoever draws the longest straw . . ." Virginia Jefferson Randolph to her husband, Nicholas Philip Trist, 1839, in Henry S. Randall, *The Life of Thomas Jefferson* (New York: Derby & Jackson, 1858), 349–51.

Page 42 "whereon to ruminate . . ." Jefferson to Dr. Vine Utley, March 21, 1819, Thomas Jefferson Papers, Library of Congress.

Page 47, year 1817 in Timeline "illimitable freedom of the human mind." Jefferson to William Roscoe, December 27, 1820, Thomas Jefferson Papers, Library of Congress.

Bibliography

Books

Betts, Edwin M., ed. *Thomas Jefferson's Garden Book.* Philadelphia: American Philosophical Society, 1944 (rep. 1999).

Betts, Edwin M. and James A. Bear Jr., eds. *The Family Letters of Thomas Jefferson.* Charlottesville: University Press of Virginia, 1966 (rep. 1986).

Fowler, Damon Lee, ed. *Dining at Monticello: In Good Taste and Abundance.* Charlottesville, Virginia: Thomas Jefferson Foundation, 2005.

Hatch, Peter J. *"A Rich Spot of Earth": Thomas Jefferson's Revolutionary Garden at Monticello.* Charlottesville, Virginia: Thomas Jefferson Foundation and Yale University Press, 2012.

Jackson, Donald Dean, ed. *Letters of the Lewis and Clark Expedition with Related Documents, 1753–1854.* Second Edition. Urbana: University of Illinois Press, 1978.

Monticello: A Guidebook. Charlottesville, Virginia: Thomas Jefferson Foundation, 2008.

Stanton, Lucia. *"Those Who Labor for My Happiness": Slavery at Thomas Jefferson's Monticello.* Charlottesville: University of Virginia Press, 2012.

Stein, Susan R. *The Worlds of Thomas Jefferson at Monticello.* New York: Harry N. Abrams, 1993.

Thomas Jefferson's Monticello. Charlottesville, Virginia: Thomas Jefferson Foundation, 2009.

Online Resources

The Monticello Web site, includes resources on almost every topic related to Jefferson and his plantation, including a virtual tour of Monticello, a Thomas Jefferson encyclopedia, a book list for further reading, and information for planning your visit to the site. http://monticello.org

Children and their teachers will enjoy exploring the Monticello classroom on the Web at http://classroom.monticello.org.

Thomas Jefferson's correspondence held by the Library of Congress can be viewed in its original manuscript form online at http://memory.loc.gov/ammem/collections/jefferson_papers.

The Thomas Jefferson Papers: An Electronic Archive includes many electronic versions of original Jefferson documents in the collection of the Massachusetts Historical Society. The archive allows users to see the original pages of the "Garden Book," the "Farm Book," architectural drawings, and other Jeffersonian manuscripts. http://www.masshist.org/thomasjeffersonpapers.

The Family Letters Project features letters between Jefferson's immediate and extended family. http://retirementseries.dataformat.com.

Acknowledgments

It takes a village to produce a book about Jefferson and Monticello. For assistance, expertise, and excellent suggestions, I am grateful to Susan Stein, Diane Ehrenpreis, Sara Bon-Harper, Jeff Looney, Eric Johnson, Peggy Cornett, Gabriele Rausse, Bob Self, Ann Lucas, Christa Dierksheide, Jodi Frederiksen, Anna Berkes, Jennifer Strotz, and especially Cinder Stanton. Sarah Allaback guided the process every step of the way.

Index

Note: Page references in italics refer to illustrations.

A
air-closets, 4
alcove bed, 3

B
Bacon, Edmund, 18
bathrooms, 4
blacksmiths, *12*, 13, 27
books, 7, 36–38, *37*
book stand, revolving, 7
breakfast, 8, 10
Brown, John, 22

C
Campeachy chair, 41–42
canals, 20–21
chamber pots, 4
charcoal, making, 27
child care, 40
clothing, 3–4, 22

Colbert, Burwell, 2, 8, 10, 38–39
coopers, 25–26

D
Declaration of Independence, v, 7, 24, 36, 46
desk, 4–5
Dick (mockingbird), 7–8, *9*
dinner, 38–39
Divers, George and Martha, 30, 34–35, 41
dogs, 17
door-opening mechanism, 41
drum carding machine, 22
dumbwaiter, 16

E
Eppes, Francis, 8, 17, 22, 24
Eppes, Mary Jefferson, 8, 46

F
"Farm Book," 25
filing presses, 6
flying shuttles, 24
food at Monticello, 30, 33–34, 38–39
foot soaking, 2–3
Fossett, Edith, 10, 27, 33–34, 38–39
Fossett, Joseph, *12*, 13

G
Gillette, Agnes, 24
Gillette, Barnaby, 25–26
Gillette, Edward, 4
Gillette, Gill, 17
Gillette, Israel, 22
gunpowder, 20, 22, 28–29

H
Hemings, Harriet, 24
Hemings, John, 10, 16